The Book of Why

Designer: Celina Carvalho
Production Manager: Alexis Mentor

Library of Congress Cataloging-in-Publication Data has been applied for.
ISBN: 0-8109-5987-9

Translated by Gita Daneshjoo
Originally published in France as *Le Livre des Pourquoi*

Published in 2006 by Abrams Books for Young Readers,
an imprint of Harry N. Abrams, Incorporated
115 West 18th Street
New York, NY 10011
www.abramsbooks.com

Originally published in French by Editions de La Martinière Jeunesse

Printed and bound in France - L 98881a
10 9 8 7 6 5 4 3 2 1

Abrams is a subsidiary of

LA MARTINIÈRE
G R O U P E

The Book of Why

Martine Laffon
Hortense de Chabaneix

Illustrations by
Jacques Azam

Contents

9

Why do parents always want children to clean up after themselves?

Maybe children don't always clean up after themselves because, deep down, they hope that someone will do it for them!

Not all of us share the same idea of tidiness, and yet we all spend a lot of time picking up after ourselves and putting stuff away. Much like the way we organize our belongings, our brains categorize all the information they receive, sorting similar objects together, like shirts with shirts and books with books.

The reason the brain categorizes information this way is so we can retain it better. If we kept our socks in the refrigerator with the pots and pans, there would probably be something seriously wrong with our brain.

And yet, out of laziness, we sometimes put our socks away with other things that don't belong. That's how disorder begins. The problem is that parents often equate a messy room with an messy brain. And they believe a messy brain means that it's difficult to learn and perform well in school.

They have a point there. Putting thing away, even if we use a syst that only makes sense to u leads to better organizatio and greater success in lif and work. Oddly enough, this starts with little thing like cleaning your room.

Why do people cry?

A fierce wind or a great fright, a fly in your face or feelings of sadness, an aggressive bug or throbbing pain: It's all the same for your body's tear factory! This factory doesn't distinguish between physical or psychological pain. So how does the whole mechanism work and where do tears come from?

Imagine a fancy car whose cleaning fluid appears at the touch of a button to make even the tiniest stain on the windshield disappear. Much like this car, your eye is uniquely designed to prevent any kind of foreign element from clouding your vision. Your eye's windshield is the transparent membrane that covers and protects the cornea. Tears are your very own cleaning fluid. And your eyelids are your windshield wipers.

This amazing factory produces, on average, half a teaspoon of tears per day, flowing regularly but never too much. But when your eyes are irritated, they produce tears continually until things go back to normal.

When you're stuffed up, and your eyes and nose can't absorb everything, tears roll down your cheeks.

So why hold back? Crying is good for you. Tears are one of the best ways of cleansing the body and keeping your vision clear!

Why are dessert plates smaller than dinner plates?

In the old days, rich families used to change plates at least six times during the course of a meal. Nowadays, even though we change them far less often, it is considered polite to eat dessert from a different plate than the one you use for your appetizer or entrée.

For most people it is preferable to keep distinct tastes separate and not mix them up on the same plate.

But why are dessert plates small? So small that there's barely enou room to fit three scoops of chocolate ice cream?

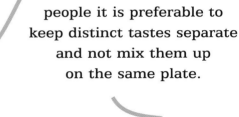

Can you even see the dessert?

Dessert comes at the end of the meal, so we can't stuff ourselves with apple pie, cupcakes, or other delicious treats the way we would at the beginning of a meal, when our stomachs are empty. The size of the dessert plate is, in fact, directly proportional to appetite.

Soup and similar dishes provide us with nourishment. But dessert is a pleasure that has nothing to do with hunger. So, if you want a big dessert plate, there's only one solution: Eat your meal backward!

Why does it rain?

When the weatherman says to expect rain, you shouldn't always take his word for it. Nobody knows for sure what the weather will be like tomorrow, let alone in two hours. So, why does it rain?

The air is in constant motion around the earth; it moves from colder to warmer places. Warm air is light and high in the ?, whereas cold air tends to be heavier and therefore lower. Because the water from oceans, rivers, and lakes is constantly evaporating, the air is full of water vapor invisible to the eye.

When air passes over cold ground, it cools and gets heavier. Instead of rain, smaller drops appear. This is how fog and dew are formed.

When cold air comes into contact with warm air, the warm air rises and the water vapor it holds becomes a cloud. When the drops of water become too heavy for the cloud to carry, they fall, and that's when you see rain!

Why does it rain every time I decide to leave the house?

Though the explanation of this phenomenon is simple, weather patterns can change in a moment's notice. Wind is unpredictable, and it's not always easy to know how strong a cold or warm front will be.

Even though meteorologists are using more and more sophisticated computers to do their work, weather forecasting remains a very complex practice.

13

Where do diseases come from?

People have long been curious about the origins of diseases.

In western medicine, diseases are grouped into four general categories. The first includes diseases caused by foreign agents, such as an insect, a virus, bacteria, pollution, or even bad food. Diseases in this category include measles, the flu, AIDS, and allergies.

The second group is diseases caused by an internal disorder—the body's functions are thrown off balance, and cells start to deteriorate and eventually self-destruct. Diabetes and cancer are included in this group.

The last two categories are diseases caused by "accidents" that occur at conception: these are called genetic and chromosomal diseases. Cystic fibrosis, for example, is a genetic disease caused by gene mutations.

GRRR

Because chromosomes exist in pairs, chromosomal diseases occur when there is an extra or missing chromosome on one of the twenty-three pairs normally present in the body. A person with Down's Syndrome has three chromosomes on the twenty-first chromosomal pair, instead of two.

Even though we have many built-in resisters to certain diseases, it's best to limit the risks of contracting them by adopting good hygiene and respecting our bodies. After all, "an ounce of prevention is worth a pound of cure!"

Why am I afraid of the dark?

Because you can't
see anything in the dark, that's
why! You're not a cat, after all. Your
eyes need a minimum of light
to focus on and decipher your
surroundings.

Leave the door
open! Turn on the hallway light!
Don't close the blinds! Everyone has
a preferred method for avoiding
complete darkness.

Many
people develop a fear of the
dark from seemingly normal
things. For example, when a baby falls
asleep in his mother's arms and wakes up
a crib in a dark room. Or when you wake
the dark to find your head at the foot
of the bed where your feet should be,
which can be very disorienting!

Or when you
are trying to find the
bathroom in the dark, but
can't remember which door
is the right one.

Poor
eyesight and memory
aren't the only problems that
are exacerbated by the dark. Our
ears are affected too—the dark seems
to amplify even the faintest shuffling
of leaves or creaks in the floorboards.
And in a drowsy state, we aren't in
full possession of our faculties
and can easily lose our
bearings.

Although
some children freely express
their fear of the dark, adults tend
to hide it. But some of them still
keep a light on at night!

15

Why do children always have to obey?

Don't play with matches, don't eat candy, brush your teeth, go to bed . . . What a pain!

But have you ever noticed, on those nature shows on TV, a mama lion holding her cub by the skin of his neck to keep him away from predators? Or a mama monkey forcing her young one to remain still while she removes her fleas?

That's because the offspring of both humans and animals don't know what's good for them at birth. It's their parents who teach them how nourish themselves, bathe, and integra into their environment. Until we acqui our own survival skills, our parents must teach us and show us how to live our lives safely.

Think of it as the "Law of Love." The most crucial role a parent can play is to give children the strength to live independent lives and the tools to assimilate with the society at large.

Here's a word of advice: The quicker you master the life lessons taught by your parents, the less they will seem like obligations!

16

Why don't we all worship the same god?

To some people, there is only one god, and for others, there are many gods and goddesses. To some people, their god is holy, but for others, gods can be perceived as evil.

In ancient times, the Greeks worshipped Zeus, the ruler of the gods. To Romans, Jupiter was the ruler of gods and men. The Egyptians had twelve powerful gods. Today, around 80 percent of people in the world have a religion, but they pray to many different gods.

Jews, Christians, and Muslims believe that there is only one creator of the world and of men. Hindus believe that Brahma, Shiva, and Vishnu are the three great divinities. It's also possible to believe in the same god but worship him differently, depending on your religion.

Why don't we all have the same god? No one knows for sure what god is really like, so everybody imagines him in his or her own way. For this reason, it's impossible for all of us to share the same idea of god.

Each religion has its own rites. They tell us how, where, and when to pray; what to eat, what is forbidden; and how to dress to always be in accordance with our god c gods. Choosing which god to believe ir often depends on your culture and the country you're from. There are few Christians in Asia, for example, and few Hindus in the West.

Why do we **fall** out of love?

The poets have long declared that love lasts forever, but we express love in so many different ways: friendship, affection, admiration, familial love, romantic love . . .

In theory, the only love that lasts a lifetime is the unconditional love a parent has for a child. When we grow up, we all go on to love someone else.

We can't help the fact that we grow up and get older. Differences between people tend to increase as time goes on. We make new friends, develop an interest in something that only yesterday seemed boring . . .

Basically, we are constantly changing, and our feelings change as well. For instance, your best friend can become your worst enemy if he jeopardizes your friendship by humiliating you. Or the two of you can drift apart if you don't share the same outlook on life.

It's always sad when a friendship comes to an end. But we also can accept people just as they are and get closer to them. It's all about trust— trust in yourself and in others.

Traitor!

I don't love you anymore!

You betrayed me!

19

How does the sky make noise?

No, thunder isn't the sound of angels bowling or an accident occurring between two clouds, though it may seem that way. The sky's ferocious noises are actually caused by specific meteorological phenomena.

When it's very hot outside or when a mass of cool, dry air meets a warm, humid air mass, huge thunderclouds form. Inside these clouds, swirls of air movement push water droplets upward. As temperatures get colder at the higher altitude, water freezes to become ice. Because they're heavy, these bits of ice begin to fall and turn into water droplets again, which descend from the clouds as rain.

Pipe down up there!

Within a cloud, water droplets and ice particles bump into each other, producing heat, light, and electric flashes: This is called lightning. The intense heat produced by a lightning bolt causes the air around it to explode with a tremendous roar: This is thunder. Because the speed of light is more than a thousand times faster than the speed of sound, we see lightning flashes before hearing the roar of thunder, unless we are very close to the center of the storm.

It is estimated that more than forty thousand storms occur on the earth each day. Incredible, but true!

Why can't we all be world champions?

World champion: What an incredible dream! Whether you win at soccer, cycling, chess, or anything else, what a thrill it would be to see your name in print, appear on TV, and sign autographs.

Though we train ourselves, push ourselves, work hard for years on end . . . It's still not good enough! Not everyone can be a world champion!

We aspire to be someone exceptional or do something unique, but despite our best efforts, we still may not succeed. We might simply lack the physical aptitude or intellectual capacity needed to get where we want to be. Or maybe the goal we set for ourselves is too high.

It's better to have your feet planted firmly on the ground than bounce from failure to failure, and it's best to evaluate your own capabilities and limitations before setting a goal.

In ancient Greece, the wise men advised people to act within their bounds, and not to set their sights too high or too low. After all, it's perfectly fine to be the champion of your own world!

21

What's inside of a hill?

A merry group of goblins who dig up tunnels and frighten moles? No, seriously, we asked geologists—scientists who study the earth's changes—what can be found inside a hill!

It took seven hundred million years for the earth to appear as it does today. The earth's surface looks different depending on where you are. In the United States, for example, the surface is composed of mountains, plateaus, hills, plains, and even some desert.

Hills actually used to be tall mountains that were created during the earth's formation, but whose rocks and rugged peaks became eroded over millions of years by wind, water, and cold. So, in a sense, they shrank. In fact, some hills measure less than five hundred feet tall and are as flat as a pancake.

The surface of the earth isn't fixed; it evolves, imperceptibly, over millions of years, and new surfaces are formed.

As for those little goblins inside the hill? Nonsense. There are only rocks, rocks, and more rocks, both inside and out!

Here I am! Me too!

Who decided that a day would be **divided** into **twenty-four** hours?

It's easy to read the time on a watch or clock; but a long time ago, people lived without such devices. The sun was used to tell time during the day. But how did people tell time at night?

The astronomers of ancient Egypt created the hours of the night by observing the stars. They noted that, like the sun, the stars rose in the east and set in the west. To observe them more easily, they divided up the sky, like a big cake, into thirty-six portions, also called sequences.

C'mon guys! It's time!

We're coming!

They also noted that one of these stars did not move—the North Star—and that other stars rotated around it. They decided to use it as a point of reference.

When observing the summer sky, the ancient Egyptian astronomers noted that only twelve portions of the sky crossed the North Star. So they assigned each of these equal portions one hour, or twelve hours for the whole night. They figured that the day would be no different and allocated a period of twelve hours for the daytime as well. A twenty-four-hour day was born.

Scientists have even discovered sundials on tombstones dating from 3000 BCE, which relied on this measure of time.

Why don't animals live as long as humans?

For every species, the aging process is "programmed" in advance, but this process can be disrupted by a host of foreign elements such as diseases that can shorten life expectancy.

Mayflies are insects whose larvae dwell at the bottom of a lake for two to three years, but live less than an hour as adults.

The world's oldest known turtle died in 1965 at the age of at least one hundred and eighty-eight. We know this because Captain Cook gave the turtle to the royal family of Tonga in either 1773 or 1777.

Scientists believe that man's natural life span is one hundred and twenty years though, due to illness and diseases, few people live that lon Along with turtles and elephants, humans are likely to live longer than most of the earth's creatures.

Thanks to progress in medicine and better standards of living, the life expectancy of humans increased more in the last century than in the previous five thousand years!

But this is true only for so-called developed countries. In areas such as southern Africa, where AIDS has infected mor than 10 percent of the population, life expectancy has decreased by sixteen years in the past quarter century.

Why are people sometimes mean?

Anyone can be mean. Being mean is a voluntary act, in which one person purposefully hurts or harms another. We're not born mean; we decide to be mean.

Anger usually triggers meanness and cruelty. The feeling arises unexpectedly and can be difficult to control. Just like that, without thinking, words, blows, and yelling can explode forth, as if you are thundering volcano. And violence beg more violence and yelling, followed quickly by tears of sadness, helplessness, and guilt.

We can't love everyone, just as we can't understand and accept everything. To avoid explosions, a pressure cooker is equipped with an escape valve to let off excess steam. We humans use words to do the same thing. Talking about our feelings, asking for an explanation, or even asking ourselves, "How did I get in this state?" often helps us decompress and avoid hurtful words and outbursts.

Wait, hold on, I'm the pitbull!

How do airplanes fly?

Many people have dreamed for centuries of being able to soar through the air, see the sun up close, and gain a bird's-eye view of the earth beneath us. And yet it's taken us century after century to figure out that simply attaching wings to our backs isn't enough to fly like a bird!

After years of observation and exploration, mankind has discovered that even though air is invisible, it contains elements of force and pressure without which lift-off wouldn't be possible. And it's this pressure that an airplane uses to fly.

When an airplane starts to accelerate, the air around its wings is divided into two parts, moving at two different speeds. Because wings are slightly curved on top, the air that passes over them is pushed upward, and an area of low pressure is created. Meanwhile, the opposite action takes place underneath. Air passing under the wings thrusts downward, exerting higher pressure on the wing, which creates lift. The combination of both these actions is what helps lift and push an airplane toward the sky.

Thus, an airplane can take off and maintain its altitude.

Failed again!

27

Why do some children suck their thumbs?

Sucking your thumb gives immediate satisfaction, and it's not unusual to see babies doing it in their mothers' wombs.

Sucking is important to babies because that's how they nourish themselves. So it's easy to see how this natural gesture can become a source of satisfaction, calmness, and serenity between feeding times.

In time, sucking one's thumb becomes reflexive. The majority of children give up the habit around the age of seven, known as the "age of reason" to child behaviorists. It's also around this age that adult teeth begin to appear. At this stage, sucking one's thumb can lead to deformations of the teeth and palate, as well as difficulty with pronunciation.

The "age of reason" also marks the time when a child feels ready to grow up and become more independent. So the child will naturally give up a habit he or she formed as a baby.

But don't panic! Seven years old isn't an absolute age limit for sucking your thumb. It's not abnormal for you to continue the habit after this age; it just means you're not ready to quit, that's all!

What makes the wind?

Trade Wind, North Wind, Mistral, Diablo, Sirocco, Willy-Willy, Zephyr: All of the one hundred and fifty winds that blow on the earth were named after the area they come from and/or their unique characteristics.

The ancients believed in divine intervention: When storms and hurricanes occurred, it meant that the gods were angry, and refreshing reezes signified the gentle breathing of a sleeping goddess. It wasn't until the seventeenth century that the great thinkers Galileo, Pascal, and Torricelli discovered that wind was more than just a simple breeze.

The temperature of the air depends on the intensity of the sun's rays. Wind comes from cold areas, where the air is heavier, and blows toward warmer areas, where air is lighter. The greater the difference in pressure between the cold and warm air currents, the stronger the wind.

It's the god of wind's little brother . . .

So why is wind invisible? Because wind is a mixture of clear, odorless gases and microscopic specks of dust, all of which are invisible to the naked eye.

When the air is heavy with rain or sand, we can sometimes see the wind moving, but most of the time we can only feel it or hear it moaning, howling, or hissing!

29

Why do most kids like chocolate and **not** spinach?

Enjoying what you eat depends on a number of related factors: odor, taste, sensation, and culture. Your body's "olfactory and taste center" is a kind of internal computer of taste located in the brain which analyzes and interprets information sent by the hundreds of millions of sensors in the nose, palate, and tongue.

Leaf vegetables like lettuce and spinach give off a bitter taste when they are cooked, which some people find unpleasant. But when they're sweetened with a sauce of your liking, they can be delicious! When it comes to chocolate, everything depends on the recipe. Try taking a bite of a cocoa bean and you'll see how bitter it can be!

Sour and bitter are not vital to our health, and our enjoyment of them depends on our particular olfactory sensors and the way our tastes have developed.

Tastes are divided into four broad categories—sweet, salty, sour, and bitter—and all of them are closely linked with memory.

Did you know that the taste sensors on your tongue are called taste buds? They respond to different tastes depending on where they're located on your tongue: The taste buds on the tip of the tongue are the most sensitive to sweet flavors. Further down, the sides of the tongue are sensitive to salt. Behind those, taste buds are sensitive to sour tastes and, all the way in the back, bitter.

Why do earthquakes occur in some places and not in others?

Our good old earth is not as stable as you might think. Things shift and crack on its surface and move around underneath the surface.

Deep within the earth's crust—the rocky shell that contains the planet's soil—lies a layer of hot, liquid rock nearly two thousand miles thick: magma. Earthquakes originate in the area between the earth's crust and these layers of magma.

The earth's crust is divided into twenty or so pieces, called tectonic plates, that float on the surface of the magma and move around at a rate of half an inch to an inch a year. These plates can move apart, slide closer together, and rub up against each other. The collision of two plates can result in tremendous friction. When the pressure is too great, the tectonic plates tear or rapidly change position.

These sudden movements generate vibrations, called seismic waves, which force their way up to the earth's surface, causing the ground to shake.

The space between two tectonic plates is called a fault. Earthquakes are much more likely to occur along these faults than in the areas that are in the middle of a plate. There are maps which locate the plates and faults along the earth's surface, so you can tell which zones are at the greatest risk for earthquakes.

Why do stars shine in the sky?

Since the dawn of time, a lot has been said about stars. Some of our distant ancestors thought that stars were pinned to the sky, as immobile and eternal as gods. Others thought that they were little holes created for rain to pass through.

Nowadays, we know that stars—like the sun, which is only one of the 200 billion stars in our galaxy—are born, live several million years, and then die out.

Stars are gigantic balls of burning gas (their temperature can reach more than 10,000 degrees F). These balls of gas give off enough energy to produce light. That's why stars shine.

However, a large number of warm air bubbles are constantly floating around in our atmosphere. If they float in front of a star, the air bubbles steal the star's light, making it appear less luminous in the sky.

Astronomers think that each star has two luminosities; apparent luminosity is the one we can see on a starry night. It varies based on the location from which we view it. Absolute luminosity belongs to the star itself and varies depending on its size. No matter where we see the star from, this luminosity never changes.

Why is the sky blue?

Poets have long extolled the pristine beauty of a blue sky on a warm summer day. But did you know that we actually see the sky through a 300-mile-thick barrier? This is the earth's atmosphere.

The earth's atmosphere is a layer of gas that makes up the air that we breathe. Think of it as a giant scarf that wraps around the planet, protecting it from the sun's rays. This gaseous layer is what makes the sky appear blue. Of the seven colors found in light from the sun, the atmosphere's gas molecules only absorb one—blue—which gets scattered throughout the sky.

The sky turns red during a sunset because at that time we're farther away from the sun. The sun's light must pass through a dense atmospheric layer. The red light scatters less than blue light in the thicker atmosphere, so the light in the direction of the sun appears reddish.

But don't let the atmosphere prevent you from enjoying the sky's view. No matter what is composed of, the sky is always beautiful.

Can someone steal my soul while I sleep?

Only in science fiction movies can bad guys enter the subconsciousnesses of good guys while they sleep. In reality, the brain remains active while we sleep, and besides, no one can get into your head. But what is the brain doing during this time?

First, it tells the nervous system to be on the lookout. This marks the period of light sleep. Next, it tells an army of different cells to restore the body: muscles, skin, bones, etc. Above all, it lets the body grow, because it is at this particular moment, and this moment only, that the growth hormone is secreted. This is the period of slow, deep sleep.

Finally, the brain refreshes itself, regroups and tries to resolve outstanding problems: This is when dreaming occurs, marking the phase of REM (rapid eye movement) sleep.

Taken together, these various phases of sleep total nearly two hours, and, depending on our needs, are repeated three, four, or even five times a night!

Forget about robbers or strangers; the images that flash before us while we sleep are merely feelings, emotions, and events of the day that reappear in new ways that often help us to better understand them.

35

Why do I get carsick?

If riding in a car makes you nauseous, it's usually because you're not the one driving it.

In a moving car, your brain processes information that it didn't ask for. It's almost as though you're functioning without your brain's permission, because the brain is the one that should be giving the orders.

Next, our eyes can't focus properly, because our heads are bobbing around every which way, due to the speed at which the car is moving. So the brain is receiving confusing information. Strike two!

So when we're in a moving car, the receptors and sensors in our ears, eyes, and feet send unsolicited information to the brain which it has trouble processing, resulting in carsickness.

We all have tiny internal receptors in our ears. They tell our brains when to reposition our heads. Vibrations, turns, and accelerations on the road trigger these receptors, and our brains experience difficulty registering this new information. Strike one!

Finally, the pressure sensors embedded in the soles of our feet help us process the ground beneath us and maintain our balance and stability. But in a car, our feet aren't touching the ground, which is in constant motion . . . So it's impossible for our brains to correctly analyze our surroundings. Third and final strike!

Emergency, stop the car! I'm carsick!

Why do flowers smell good?

There's no way for a planted flower to go off in search of a husband to make baby flowers! Even flowers that are equipped with both male and female reproductive organs can't fertilize themselves.

Pollen must be transported to another flower of the same species for fertilization to occur. Flowers must rely on what nature has placed at their disposal to make this happen: wind and insects.

The most timid flowers, those which usually go unnoticed, rely on the wind to scatter their pollen. These are considered anemophilous.

Pshhh

Others, which are referred to as entomophilous, are real flirts! They lure insects with their bright colors and enticing perfumes. Insects approach them and easily adhere to the flowers because pollen is sticky. Like the gluttons they are, insects move from flower to flower, collecting pollen and transporting it to other flowers, thereby achieving cross-pollination.

A flower's perfume doesn't attract only insects, however . . . For thousands of years, humans have tried to reproduce these intoxicating odors to win favors from their gods and neighbors!

What is infinity?

Infinity . . . what a strange concept. It stretches on and on like a long snake, without end.

Infinity is a difficult idea to comprehend, because everything around us has boundaries: our house has two floors, the garden extends from the tall oak tree to the neighbor's fence, and walking home from school takes five minutes.

But it's more complicated farther from our world. What lies beyond the billions of galaxies? Where does space—that great expanse of the universe beyond earth—end? Does it ever stop somewhere?

For centuries, scientists have constructed powerful telescopes, perfecting them over the years in order to see farther and farther away. Space is so big that it's impossible to know exactly how far it goes, or if there even is an end. The word infinity is used to describe something that has no limits.

Maybe one day we'll figure out where space begins and ends, and discover that it isn't infinite. But for now, the answer keeps its (endless) distance!

Why do our teeth fall out when we're little?

Dolphins are born with all their teeth, but because they have so many (some species have up to 250 teeth) it doesn't matter if they fall out. Snakes a crocodiles can lose and replace all the teeth up to twenty-five times in the course of their lifetimes!

As for humans, we have different kinds of teeth assigned to specific functions. Our teeth grow in two successive stages: baby teeth and adult teeth.

Hello there, I'm the tooth fairy!

These two stages of teeth are formed in the interior of the gums after the human embryo's second month of life. Their roots grow until the first teeth poke through the gums, about six months after birth. At this age, a child's digestive system is ready to absorb solid food.

But the jaw doesn't reach its full size until fifteen years of age. Before then, all those adult teeth would never fit in such a small mouth!

When the first four molars appear, the tooth fairy will soon be making her first visit. Baby teeth fall out to make room for adult teeth. All of our teeth are fully grown by the time we turn fifteen, except for wisdom teeth, which either grow much later, or never at all.

Why are witches always mean in children's stories?

With their hooked noses, clawed fingers, hairy chins, and tousled hair, storybook witches put curses on people, eat children, and transform princes into toads.

They do their job well: Witches scare us in stories!

Reading scary stories helps us blow off steam and rid ourselves of bad thoughts. For example, we may secretly hope to unload the burden of a little sister or a mother who complains and punishes us.

Isn't it comforting to imagine your little sister getting cooked in the bubbling brew in the witch's cauldron? Better her than you, right?

Witches are wicked because it's always the nice guy who wins in the end. The reader of a book always imagines himself as the superhero or heroine who does good deeds, as opposed to the cruel, wicked witch. In a way, the witch makes us want to be a better person.

Then again, if the roles were reversed, and the witch became the friendly heroine of the story, we would likely have no problem identifying with her!

Why are some people afraid to walk under a ladder?

Maybe we avoid walking under a ladder because we're afraid of getting hit by a can of paint or some kind of unidentifiable object; but some people believe walking under a ladder brings bad luck.

These people fear that walking through the triangular space formed by the leaning ladder, the edge of the wall, and the ground will break up the three points corresponding to the three sides of a triangle. For many cultures, the number three signifies perfection and shouldn't be disrupted in any way. We call this way of thinking *superstition*.

Superstition comes from the Latin word *superstitio*, which means "standing over" with an added element of men

The following actions are considered superstitious: a black cat crossing your path, having thirteen people at the same table, spilling salt from a saltshaker, finding a four-leaf clover, or playing lottery on Friday the thirteenth. Being superstitious means believing that actions, colors, animals, days, and objects can be lucky or unlucky, and can alter the normal course of events.

Careful!

It's sort of like giving everyday things magical powers . . . If only!

How can we go on living when someone we love dies?

We can't prevent the death of loved ones. Because we love them so, the pain of their loss can be excruciating, and we may think that there's no end to the sadness we feel. But they are the ones who cease living, not you.

Our entire history is made up of people whose lives, at one moment or another, came to an end. But they will always remain a part of our families and our lives, of who we are now and who we will someday become.

Nobody knows in advance when they will pass away. Nor does anybody really know what happens to us after we die.

Death is scary, precisely because it's the greatest unknown. But we can help one another overcome this fear by making the most out of life: meeting new people, loving each other, and preparing ourselves for what's to come.

The death of one person doesn't end the life of another. On the contrary, it should renew our will to live life to the fullest and to never forget those we have lost.

43

Why did prehistoric people have so much hair?

Because prehistoric people did not have as much clothing or shelter as we do today, body hair was essential to their survival. But nowadays we live in a much warmer climate, and our fur slowly began to disappear during the course of our evolution. So why is it that we still have more than a hundred million hairs on our bodies?

With the exception of our eyelashes, eyebrows, and the hair on our heads, our body hair at birth is extremely fine. It becomes thicker and darker during puberty. The rate of its growth and how long it remains varies by age, gender, and where it grows on our bodies.

Each hair follicle is connected to a specialized gland called a sebaceous gland. This little duct secretes an oily substance—sebum—which softens and waterproofs skin, prevents bacteria from penetrating the surface, and helps to maintain a stable body temperature. What a system!

When you're scared, angry, cold, or emotional, a little muscle on the hair contracts, causing goose bumps!

Several million years ago, when we were still covered in hair, our body hair even helped to deter our enemies! And guess what else? The stiff spikes on the spine of a hedgehog are also hairs!

Why do some parents work all the time?

If you need something, call us . . .

gotta go . . .

to work!

They leave the house at eight in the morning and often don't get home until after seven o'clock, five days a week . . . Wouldn't it be nicer if our parents were always on vacation?

What good does it do to work around the clock if they never see their kids? That is no way to live, no matter how much they love their jobs!

But sometimes there's no way around it. Work means a salary, and a salary means money to buy the things we need to eat, take care of ourselves, have fun, get around, raise kids, and send them to school so that they, too, can get good jobs and make a good living . . . This is the way our economy works.

For our distant ancestors more than thirty thousand years ago, a few days of hunting or gathering per week was enough to feed the entire household. But today we could never depend on hunting and gathering for our livelihood!

But being a slave to a job and coming home every night weighed down by files and papers isn't the solution. Striking a balance between time devoted to work and time spent as a family will give parents the peace of mind to enjoy pastimes such as chasing butterflies and gathering flowers . . . with their children.

46

How do we know what we want to be when we grow up?

In the old days, we didn't question what kind of job we would have. We just followed family tradition. If you were the son of a farmer, you would become a farmer as well. And in the wealthier, titled families, the oldest son took over the fields, the second-born son went off to war, and the youngest joined the church.

As for girls, they would be married off to sons of other families from the same social class without anyone asking for their input. Only in rare instances could you escape the destiny that awaited you.

Today, everything has changed. There are so many fields of study and various jobs available that the choices are overwhelming.

The lucky ones have already chosen a career path. They are so passionate about a certain profession that they're prepared to move mountains to get there. Others make a career decision during the course of their studies, or later in life.

Curiosity is hardly a flaw when it comes to your future. The more questions you ask about the kind of work people around you do, the more ideas you will have about what you might want to do yourself.

There is no miracle solution for figuring out what kind of career to pursue, but one thing is certain: The better your grades are, the greater your choices will be.

47

Why do we resemble monkeys?

Is there a genetic reason some people are so good at making monkey faces? This is a question which scientists have been asking for 150 years, since the first human fossils—dating from several million years ago—were discovered. Do chimpanzees and humans share a common origin? The answer appears to be yes.

There are undoubtedly some surprising similarities between monkeys and humans: Larger monkeys stand upright, use their hands, and know how to make tools and adapt to new environments, just like us.

On the other hand, humans are rather incapable by comparison. We have difficulty swinging from branch to branch!

The visible, external differences between us include the shape of our faces, body hair, the way in which we stand upright, and also our behavior with other members of the species. Monkeys communicate among themselves by using signs and grunts of varying intensity. Humans speak using articulated language.

Hoo! Hoo! Hoo!

But there is an even greater difference: Humans are conscious of being conscious. When they act, they know what they're doing and why. Huma[n] can think, reflect, remember, and anticipa[te] what happens to them! So if humans ar[e] merely monkeys who have evolved afte[r] years and years . . . That's some evolution!

Why is there life on earth?

When the earth was formed, approximately 4.5 billion years ago, it was nothing but a great big ball of red molten rock. Millions of years elapsed before it cooled down and a cloudy exterior was created: the atmosphere.

The atmosphere is a protective covering that prevents the earth from burning during the day due to the intense heat of the sun, or from freezing at night. The atmosphere is also where all kinds of meteorological phenomena take place. In fact, a billion years after the earth was formed, rain fell continuously, creating the first oceans.

Thanks to this water and oxygen, microscopic bacteria slowly began to appear and evolved into numerous living species. The earth is the only planet in our solar system whose surface is 70 percent water.

Astronomers have observed traces of dried-up water sources on Mars, or sheets ice on Uranus, but they've never een a quantity of water sufficient to sustain life.

But who knows? Perhaps some day, far away in the universe, we may find new neighbors!

Why are some people rich and others poor?

We know that there are rich countries and poor countries, and within those countries, rich people and poor people. But has this inequality existed since the dawn of humanity?

Some people think it all started the day a man placed a fence around his little plot of land and exclaimed, "This is mine!" After that, the urge to constantly acquire more and more led to an unequal distribution of resources.

There's no more room!

The most fundamental human rights that each person is entitled to—food, lodging, work, health care, and education—are far from guaranteed. There are still many people who are starving, homeless, unemployed, lack access to medicine, or are unable to attend school.

History has shown that countries have destroyed each other to reap benefits, with no regard for the plight of the people living in the conquered nation. Usually it's because they want to gain new territories or exploit natural resources that don't belong to them.

There are many root causes of poverty, but no one should simply accept that the poor stay poor and the rich become richer. Each country should strive for a better, more equitable distribution of wealth among its inhabitants. Wealthier countries have an obligation to encourage the development of poorer countries.

Why do grandparents have gray hair?

Just like our skin color, our hair color depends on the amount of brown pigment—melanin—produced by cells to protect us from the sun's harmful rays.

The more melanin these cells contain, the darker our hair and skin are. The range of hair color is extensive, going from black to pale yellow, with everything in between.

When we get older, for example around the age of forty or so, our cells become lazier, and melanin production decreases. Hair slowly begins to lose its color, turning gray first and then white.

Some people's hair turns gray prematurely, while they're still quite young; in most cases this is due to stress or a serious emotional breakdown which shocks the system. But often it's simply because their production of melanin slowed down or stopped too soon.

We're not going to let ourselves go gray!

51

Did God really create humans?

People have been asking themselves where they came from for millions of years. Who or what gave them life? Their parents! And who gave their parents life? *Their* parents! And so on . . .

But if we could go back in time to the first human, the question would always be the same: Where did he or she come from?

Some people used to think that if we learned how the different species appeared on earth, we would finally be able to solve the riddle of where humans came from.

Nowadays, we know that there never was a first human, but many first humans, and that they came from the same species—the primates—following a long evolution of living organisms: fish, amphibians, reptiles, and then birds and mammals.

How did we pass from one species to another? That's precisely what scientists would like to know. But their theories, experiments, and observations will never answer the question of whether or not God created man.

Many different cultures and religions tell their own stories about how God created man. But their views are not necessarily in competition with those of scientists.

Actually, these groups are not even asking the same question. Scientists want to know how humans came to be. The writers of religious texts want to know why life exists, and why humans in particular exist. The authors of the Bible thought that everything that exists was created by God.

At what age do we fall in love?

There is no minimum age at which we fall in love. Loving someone or something is part of what it means to be human, and it begins at birth.

But how can we distinguish romantic love from friendship or admiration for another person? It's a question of time, reflection, and experience.

Those who yearn to become one with another person confuse love with infatuation. These people forget that love, like friendship, is built on respect, trust, and freedom. Love at first sight happens, but true love must be built over time.

It's unlikely for someone to go through life without heartbreak. But keep in mind that these heartbreaks are learning processes that push you forward to the next stage of adulthood.

And whatever happens, know that love in all its forms is what gives us meaning in life, at any age.

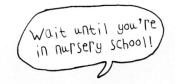
Wait until you're in nursery school!

But age doesn't matter!

Why does fire burn?

Our distant ancestor Homo erectus is credited with the discovery of fire, at least 500,000 years ago! More precisely, he learned how to start and control it, because fire has existed forever. But what is fire exactly?

Fire is a combination of light, heat, and flames, triggered by a substance that burns. This can be wood, charcoal, or gasoline, but also a blanket, book, or our hand!

Fire is like a big monster that is prepared to devour anything in its path. You can run your finger quickly through the flame of a match without feeling anything, but you can't leave it there for a second longer without burning yourself. Our skin is resistant to heat, but only up to a certain point.

Every year, hundreds of thousands of people burn themselves with varying degrees of severity. The causes are often sources of intense heat which people are not careful about: heated milk which overflows in its pan, a forgotten clothes iron, or staying out too long in the sun. Regardless of the degree of heat, getting burned is serious.

Aha!

It feels warmer over here!

Even if learning to control fire contributed greatly to our evolution as a species, there's still no excuse for acting like Vulcan or other fire gods; fire can be very dangerous!

55

Why are planets round?

Why aren't stars actually star-shaped, or planets shaped like cubes or pyramids?

Because in space, everything revolves around gravity, the force of attraction that pulls bodies toward each other.

The shape of a sphere allows all parties to be as close as possible to each other. In a cube, the corners would be at a disadvantage, because they would be farther away from the center.

So, spontaneously, bodies that are held together by gravity take on a rounded shape. It's a little like how people naturally form a circle around a street performer in order to see him better.

Why do we die?

Everything in nature deteriorates, grows old, and disappears. All living things eventually die. Scientists have tried to convince us that we can delay the aging of cells and repair them, but there's no avoiding the fact that one day we will die. So what good does it do?

Obviously, if everyone were still living after seven million years, we wouldn't have that much room left on earth. But we can't justify death merely because we don't have enough space to accommodate everyone.

Although we may never know why we die, we can at least try to come to terms with it.

Many cultures and religions believe that death does not mean the end of life. They think that even though a person physically deteriorates after death, his soul lives on, or is reincarnated, which means that he comes back as another person and lives a whole new life. This is what Hindus believe.

For people in Africa, the dead allow those still living to communicate with the world beyond.

In other religions, death is merely a pit stop on the path toward God and divinity.

Why aren't we all the same?

Dark skin, light skin; green, blue, or brown eyes: Nobody looks exactly like anybody else, not even twins. This is what genetics, or the science of genes, is about: figuring out what makes each of us unique.

Genes carry our hereditary information inside our bodies' cells. The information contained in an individual's genes is like a little book in which his or hers genetic code is written. This is what we call a genetic card.

The climate in which we live, what we eat, and the places where we live affect our physical appearance—people who live in cold climates don't look like those who live in tropical ones. But there are not specific Asian, African, or European genes.

All humans share the same genes, but some appear more frequently than others, depending on a person's race or ethnicity.

How lucky we are to be built the same way and yet still be so different from each other!

Why are tomatoes red?

Because they're fully ripe, that's why! OK, but why are they red and not, say, purple? It's actually not that simple . . .

The color of an object depends on three things: the nature of the object, the light that shines on it, and how your eyes see it.

Here's a little experiment: Light from the sun contains seven principal colors—red, orange, yellow, green, blue, indigo, and violet. What would happen if you shone the light on a tomato? The tomato, like a sponge soaking up water, absorbs all the colors except red. Only the red is reflected back to your eye. So you see the tomato as red!

Give me a break!

Now, try shining a green light on the same tomato. What happens? The tomato seems to turn black! Why? Because the green light doesn't contain any red, so the tomato doesn't reflect any color. The absence of color makes it black.

Why do kids always want to act like grown-ups?

Adults don't always like it when kids try to imitate them. But though they may not realize it, grown-ups also imitate their elders: their parents; their heroes, either real or imaginary; famous people; religious figures; or athletes.

But why would someone want to imitate someone else? Today, psychologists tell us that kids need role models to help them shape their own identities.

They learn a number of important things from adults, like how to tell right from wrong, and what's acceptable or dangerous.

When they get older, children continue to follow the examples that have been set for them. They can either adapt them to their own ways of thinking, or reject them entirely and invent new ones.

But in the meantime, children will continue to think that grown-ups' lives are full of adventure. Whatever they're doing is always more exciting!

61

Why don't we all have the same skin color?

Experts see us all as having the same color skin. In some ways, they're not wrong. Seen through a microscope, all skin, regardless of color, contains cells filled with the same brown substance: melanin. Melanin is a pigment which protects us from the harmful rays of the sun. Melanin production increases in response to greater sun exposure.

Several million years ago, the first inhabitants of the earth lived in Africa, where the sun shines intensely. Their skin was very dark, because adapted to the particular climate in which they lived.

When different peoples conquered new territories in cooler continents, they no longer needed as much protection; over time, their skin lightened.

The same pigment can be found in all types of skin, but the quantity varies according to race.

Fair-skinned people love to get a suntan, but be careful! Nature may have given us natural protection, but melanin can't prevent any of us, fair- or dark-skinned, from getting sunburned. Our best protection can only be found in tubes: suntan lotion!

Chocolate, Vanilla, Vanilla-Strawberr

Why is there night and day?

Here's an interesting experiment: Bring a ball into a dark room. Place the ball on the ground in front of a flashlight. Spin the ball around and look! Only one side of the ball is illuminated. The other remains completely dark!

This is how day and night work. Imagine that the flashlight is the sun, an enormous spotlight that never shuts off, and the ball represents the earth.

The earth rotates, from west to east, at a thousand miles an hour each day; each time one side passes in front of the sun, it's daytime, but for the other half of the world, it's nighttime.

Think of it this way: It's not the sun that rises and sets. We're the ones who choose to turn our backs to the sun!

It's my turn!

No, mine!

Everyone gets his own turn!

Why do we learn things at school that seem useless?

It's not easy trying to figure out if something is useful or not! A lesson learned at school may seem useless now, but how can you be sure that it won't come in handy five years from now? What is your definition of useful knowledge, anyway? Simply learning how to read and count? Isn't there more worth learning about?

In school, we acquire indispensable knowledge about the universe, people, inventions, and many other things. Later, this base of knowledge will help us choose a profession.

Of course, some things may seem less important than others, but they are useful in that they pique our curiosity, open our minds, and give us the tools we need to learn new things, resolve problems, and adapt to new situations.

But we can't learn all of life's lessons on our own. We need professors to help us understand, explain, and retain this knowledge. This acquired knowledge helps us to communicate, think, invent, and live side-by-side in society.

Knowledge will help you to look beyond the tip of your nose!

I've got it!
Everything finally makes sense.
The universe, humanity, inventions . . .

Why do doors close?

A little window . . . a door, open to the sun . . . In the villages of yesteryear, houses didn't have many openings, not only due to cold weather and the threat of robbery, but also because a t. was charged to people based on the numb of doors and windows they had in their homes. Doors were often made in two pieces, allowing the top part to open for fresh air to circulate.

So why do doors close? Because a closed-off space is safe and intimate, giving a person the opportunity to be alone. Closing the door gives you your own little universe, and everything that belongs to you is protected inside. This way, you can shut out bad weather, robbers, strangers, or nosy people who happen to pass by!

In certain warm and humid regions, such as the Amazon rainforest, you can still find houses without doors. These houses are held up by wooden pillars, and their roofs are made of woven palm leaves. In these homes, fresh air is always welcome. And if you're looking for privacy, there's always the hammock!

Which door?

Why aren't children's stories true?

Pumpkins that transform into carriages, magic wands, and Prince Charmings—all of this isn't real? They're only stories to help children fall asleep?

That's right! Even if we cried with the heroine, cheered on the hero, sailed off on a boat full of pirates, or liberated planet Z44, the characters from these stories aren't real; they merely sprang from the imaginations of the people who wrote them.

An imaginary story will never come true. It's called fiction. The stories aren't real because the characters in them don't exist in everyday life, like you do. However, although stories aren't real, they can still more or less resemble real life.

Imagine if, starting tomorrow, all the heroes, monsters, and princesses from our stories actually came to life! What would there be left to dream about? What could we invent in our minds?

I'm quite aware that you're not real!

After all, would we really want to cross paths with a real, honest-to-goodness goblin, running wild in the streets?

Why do parents always find out when we've done something bad?

Do your parents have a "third eye," a kind of hidden camera that captures your every move when they're not there? No! Then how come they always end up knowing everything? They pay attention, that's all!

Face it: It's not that hard to figure out that you used nail polish, when there are traces of it all over the carpet! Nor is it a big mystery that you played in the hay, when it's practically spilling out of your shoes!

And even if you greet them innocently and obediently, they can't help but think that you're hiding something . . . The more you squirm, blush, or mumble when answering their questions, the more certain they will be that you've done something bad!

There's no need for a "third eye" or a hidden camera, because parents are extremely observant! But even though they can usually guess what you're up to, they can't know everything!

And in several years, when you confess certain childhood trespasses, rest assured that they're in for a big surprise!

What's the point of prayer?

A prayer is a kind of speech addressed to someone who lives in an entirely different world from the one in which we live. We can pray to God, divine beings, or to supernatural powers, as a way of communicating with them.

Each religion has its own rites with particular gestures, clothing, and sacred places of worship: temples, churches, pagodas, forests, synagogues, and mosques. There are also specified times for prayer. It's not the prayer itself which is powerful, but the person to whom it is addressed.

Whether we pray alone or in groups, prayer has a clear objective. Much like a call, it asks for a response. And one always hopes that a prayer is answered.

Hello God?? . . . I'm listening . . . Hello?

The connection is bad today.

There are many different reasons why we pray. For example, you might pray for good fortune, or to prevent misfortune, pass an exam, recover from an illness, earn money, or protect yourself from enemies.

However, in most cases, prayer is simply a dialogue with a higher power.

Why don't we all speak the same language?

Speech specialists differentiate between speech and language. Speech refers to all our means of expression—the sounds, gestures, and signs that enable humans to communicate with each other. Language is a combination of specific words that belong to a community.

French, Chinese, Berber, Inuit—we don't all speak the same language, because we all belong to different communities. However, the sounds and structure of similar words prove that some distinct languages share the same root.

Languages evolved through contact with others. French, Italian, Spanish, Sanskrit, and many others are called Indo-European languages. English is part of the Proto-Germanic language group, a subset of Indo-European. There are over a hundred different families of languages in the world.

Though speech is innate, languages are learned. People have always dreamed of speaking the same language, and some have even invented languages, often without success. English is the most widely spoken language in the world today.

We use language in order to speak; it allows us to express what we want to say. Nobody can speak on your behalf, and everyone has the right to speech, no matter what language you use to express yourself.

Why do we put people in prison?

If everything were permitted, there would be no need for justice. Everybody would do as they pleased with little regard for the welfare of others. The strong would soon enough squash the weak. That's why when someone commits a crime against someone else—robbery, violence, or even murder—that crime does not go unpunished.

One way of punishing a criminal is to deprive him of his freedom. If society decides, after judging his case, that someone is a threat to the life, security, and welfare of others, that person is put in prison for a certain amount of time, depending on the crime committed. By putting criminals behind bars, society can both protect itself and punish those who disobey the law.

Depriving a citizen of his rights as well as the freedom to move about and communicate with the outside world is considered by the courts a proper punishment for the harm inflicted on that person's victims. If the crime is severe enough that no compensation is possible, the criminal will be locked up forever. Well, at least for the rest of his life.

Why are spiders so scary?

Peeking out from their hiding places and lurking about with their eight hairy legs . . . *Eeeeeeek!* You tremble just thinking about them creeping up on you, opening their venomous fangs and biting you while you sleep!

It's true, spiders don't have a great reputation. But maybe you just need to get to know them a little better, without bias, before they can win you over!

Spiders may be carnivores, but they don't suck your blood the way mosquitoes do, which are, fortunately for us, eaten by spiders. Spiders only feed on insects.

There's no denying that spiders have venomous glands and fangs which they use to bite and immobilize their prey. But there's no need to exaggerate! Given a spider's size, the amount of venom they possess is not a lot. With the exception of the most dangerous species of spiders—which you're unlikely to encounter, since they live in faraway places—their bites are not fatal.

Need more reassurance? Are you wondering why spiders still bite us at night, when we're asleep and not bothering them in the least? Blame it on a chance encounter. The spider isn't on a mission to bite you, but when it spots your leg, how can it resist?

Why do people say that the dead go to heaven after we bury them?

People have always thought that the gods lived in the sky, high above our heads, keeping company with the mighty sun, lightning, and the stars.

Some people compare heaven to a father and the earth to a mother. Our ancestors feared that heaven would fall on their heads, an they also feared the underground, which they thought was full of evil people who held the dead hostage.

Hey, you, up there!

In the Christian faith, when someone dies, it is said that his spirit leaves th world and ascends to heaven. But it's actually just a metaphor.

In some religions, one mustn't utter god's name out of respect, so heaven is used when speaking about god.

The expression "going to heaven" is used in everyday language. But nobody actually lives in the sky after he or she is dead and buried.

Why do people feel pain?

The brain is in an ideal position for controlling pain.

The sensory receptors in our skin, muscles, veins, and internal organs respond quickly to extreme heat or cold, strong pressure, or injury and send messages from every inch of our body to the spinal cord—the nerve center which transmits information from the brain to the body—at the speed of about a hundred feet per second. When you get sick, your red and white blood cells act on the information from these receptors, causing pain.

But your sensitivity to pain depends more on memory, education, stress, and fear than on the quantity or quality of your receptors.

It's perfectly normal to hate getting a handful of dust in your eyes or going to the dentist to get your teeth cleaned; the receptors are highly concentrated in these areas, one per millimeter in the eyes or teeth!

There's no shame in feeling pain and saying something about it, but it's often difficult to express the extent of our suffering. That's why doctors have created a pain scale ranging from one to ten; the purpose is not to rank us, of course, but to better understand our pain.

75

Why do we dream?

The more we sleep, the longer our dreams are—ten, twenty, even thirty minutes in length. Sometimes we remember them, sometimes not. But it's not easy to figure out why we dream in the first place.

Some people think that dreams symbolize something profound in our lives, and that they should be interpreted in order to grasp their meaning. In antiqui for example, dreams were thought to h messages sent by gods. In Egypt, psych were summoned to interpret the drear of pharaohs.

In some traditional cultures, healers might dream the cause of an illness, as well as its cure.

Some people believe that dreams are a bit like movies: They can appear in color or black and white, each with their own set design. They express our everyday worries, fears, and desires in a unique way.

Finally, some people dream when they're awake and don't real- ize it, which you know if you've ever daydreamed in class!

Why do some people bite their nails?

There are as many answers to this question as there are people who bite their nails. An average of one person in three suffers from this habit—an entire book on the subject wouldn't be enough to explain it!

Everyone has a reason for biting their nails. But wearing gloves or painting your nails with foul-tasting nail polish is only a temporary solution to the problem. If you want to successfully kick the habit, you have to figure out why you started it in the first place.

Imagine yourself as Sherlock Holmes or any other famous detective, and try to figure out when and where you bite your nails.

Is it at home? At school? When you're alone or with others? Does the urge come about when you're bored or anxious?

If you keep track of these fateful moments, mentally or by jotting them down in a little notebook, this awful habit may in fact disappear on its own. Constantly caught in the act of biting, your unconscious will slowly lose its grip on the mutilation of your fingers!

Do plants talk to each other?

No, plants don't talk, they whisper! Haven't you ever heard them? You can hear them whispering softly in the hollows of ditches, on the riverbanks, and in the summer wind. But seriously, how could we even know if plants talk among themselves?

Some scientists say that although plants don't talk to each other, they can still exchange information by way of chemical gas emissions.

For example: "Be careful! Predators are near." Plants that are being aggressively grazed upon by animals send this gaseous signal to neighboring plants. Having heeded the warnings, these plants can then defend themselves by giving off an indigestible substance. This helps discourage animals with even the most voracious appetites!

But if they aren't being eaten, plants don't need to send their defensive signal, because they don't feel threatened.

Sometimes we forget that plants are living organisms . . . Plants can easily live without us, but we can't live without them! That's as good a reason as any for respecting them!

Why do dogs and cats hate each other?

Isn't this just a myth taken from cartoons? An animosity created by humans between pets who, in fact, have no reason to be at odds with one another?

Although both species are hunters, cats and dogs have very distinctive hunting techniques. One is known to spend hours waiting for a mouse or bird to come within paw's length. The other keeps his nose close to the ground, following the scent of his prey until he closes in on it.

In nature, fellow predators don't attack each other; rather, they ignore one another. They keep their hunting ground, and their prey, to themselves.

In farms and households, pets are well fed; they hunt as a pastime, or to impress their owners. It's no wonder that a dog would be tempted to chase after a cat, if he sees one dart across his path. It's all in the name of fun.

What about the myth people expect us to uphold?

Forget about it!

But for the most part, if dogs and cats don't bother one another, they actually get along quite well.

What good does it do to believe in God?

Before thinking about the reasons for believing in God, we should ask ourselves what we mean by "believing in God."

We can just as easily believe in Santa Claus, ghosts, or extraterrestrials. Why? For the sake of comfort, thrills, and daydreams.

Believing in God doesn't mean that you should blindly accept everything written about God. On the contrary, being a believer means that you use your intelligence and good judgment to seek the truth.

More than anything else, believing in God means wondering whether a god exists beyond the world that surrounds us, and whether what we say about him (or her or them) is true.

Does the pursuit of this truth have some kind of purpose? For some theologians (theology is the science of God), believing in God means believing in life and the energy that allows us to grow. For all of us, belief in a god or gods demands that we act in accordance with our faith.

Ohhhh!

Santa Claus!

Why are wars fought?

Violence between two groups occurs when one group steals something that the other group possesses.

In prehistoric times, our ancestors fought one another in order to seize new fertile lands in which to settle.

Nowadays, many wars are fought because of boundary disputes with neighboring countries: These are known as territorial wars.

Some people refuse to share their land with other people whose roots, culture, and religion differ from their own, so they fight in order to impose their ideas and way of life on another group.

Some groups don't rely on just their armies to fight battles, but adopt new strategies, such as terrorist attacks or taking hostages.

However, in 1945, in the aftermath of World War II, the countries of the world decided to work together to prevent more wars from happening, and pledged to help each other both economically and culturally. These countries founded the UN, the United Nations, because, as the novelist Albert Camus said, "Peace is the only battle worth waging."

Why are girls different from boys?

All the secrets of our genetic makeup are contained in the nucleus of our bodies' cells, in the form of microscopic rods called "chromosomes." Humans have forty-six chromosomes. Twenty-three of them come from your father and the other twenty-three from your mother.

When a sperm implants itself in the egg in the uterus during conception, the paternal and maternal chromosomes group together to form pairs. The twenty-third, and last, chromosomal pair is the one that determines your sex.

The sex chromosome given by your mother is always X, where-s your father's can be either X or Y. ney are called X and Y because these tters resemble their shapes. There's a 50 percent chance that the last pair will be either XX, a girl, or XY, a boy.

Hello girls!

Chromosomes going for a walk

Because your cells differ depending on whether you're a girl or a boy, not only do your visible repro-ductive organs differ, but your body functions in different ways as well.

So, is all of this just a simple matter of letters in the alphabet? Not quite. There isn't any difference between girls and boys, in general, when it comes to feelings, intelligence, and even physical force, only differences between individuals. How girls or boys grow up often depends on their families and the society in which they live.

Why do **we** get jealous?

I hate when my little sister gets to stay at home all day with my mom while I'm at school. I can't stand the idea of my best friend going to that other kid's hous for the weekend! I feel so let down when my dog pays more attention t my dad, even though I was the one who played with the dog all day long.

Hold it! Stop everything! Jealousy can ruin your relationships with others.

But the feeling is not easy to control.

Jealousy comes about when a person lacks confidence in him- or herself, thinking something like, "I'm not good enough to be loved." Jealousy describes both the heartbreak of seeing someone else enjoy something we can't have and the fear of losing what we already have.

Jealousy can be overwhelming at times; it can make us believe that things are better for everyone else.

All of us are susceptible to feeling this kind of suffering at one point or another in our lives. When we start to feel jealousy, we should make an effort to stop it in its tracks, because otherwise it can really mess u our relations with others. Worst of all, jealou: prevents us from taking care of ourselves and making the most out of what we already have.

Why are some people bald?

Each person has approximately 100,000 hairs on his head. These hairs grow at a rate of about half of an inch per month.

That means that an average of six inches of hair grows on your head each year!

The lifespan of one hair lasts anywhere from three to eight years, and it can replace itself up to fifteen times during the course of a lifetime.

When a person becomes bald, it's because their hair replacement cycle stopped too soon, and as a result, their stock of hair is depleted.

You're invited to my birthday party.

Tomorrow I'll be eight years old!

Are there many people coming?

Three, if I don't fall out before then.

Why aren't we upside down when we're on the other side of the earth?

You only think you're not upside down! Everything depends on your point of view. Seen from high up in space, the earth looks a bit like a pincushion. We, the people, are the pins, although very, very, tiny ones. Some of the pins are upside down; others are right side up or sticking out horizontally.

Gravity is what plants us firmly on the earth, like the pins on a cushion, pulling us in like a magnet. Gravity is the force that makes all bodies attract, regardless of what they are. The greater the size difference between two bodies, the stronger the attraction between the big and the small.

I feel a little dizzy.

Because the earth is round, its gravity is the same all over its surface. That's why we remain on the ground no matter where we are in the world, and why rivers flow down from mountains, or why a balloon flying overhead eventually falls back down to the ground.

Gravity is also the thing that ensures that the moon rotates around the earth and the earth around the sun, without any of them falling onto one another.

So unless you fall on your head, you will never find yourself upside down on the other side of the earth!

Why can't we stop ourselves from lying?

At around the age of two, a child may attempt a few white lies, just to make sure that his parents can't read his mind. Think of it as a rite of passage in the formation and affirmation of his personality. If you're all alone on a desert island, you can make up as many stories as you like, but these aren't considered lies. Lies require the participation of at least one other person.

A lie can either be useful or compensatory. When you know that you've done something bad and refuse to admit it out of fear of punishment or betrayal, you tell a lie that is useful to you—you omit the truth for the sake of convenience.

Candy? There's no candy here.

A compensatory lie is told when you invent or embellish a certain event in your life for the sake of making it more irresistible in the eyes of others.

It's not always easy to tell the truth. That's why sometimes it may seem easier to lie. But no matter what kind you tell, lies always lead us on a downward spiral which may eventually prove too difficult to reverse.

Truth requires courage, but it brings instant relief! It's up to you to decide which path to take!

Can wishes come true?

Have you ever seen a shooting star? They say it brings good luck! Make a wish, and it'll come true. Great, but how? To whom, exactly, do we make the wish? Who has the power to make our wishes come true? Unless luck is always on your side, there is actually little chance of all of your wishes becoming reality.

Happy New Year! Here's to your health! Good luck to the newly-weds! These types of wishes are one way of warding off bad luck. But even if we try with all our might to make these things come true, it's not always possible. We can't intervene with fate, because it doesn't depend on us. We have no control over illness or death.

But there are also the kinds of wishes that are like vows we make to ourselves—the vow to be truthful, to not cheat, or to practice non-violence. In these cases, we decide whether or not these wishes will come true.

Hello there!

One day I, too, will be a star!

Why won't our parents let us get a dog?

So who's going to take the walking fleabag out? Who's going to feed him? Who's going to watch him wh[en] you're on vacation? Who will take care of [him] when he gets sick? And who will cons[ole] him when he's all alone?

If your request to get a dog provokes an avalanche of questions from your parents, your best bet is not to insist. Obviously, your parents just aren't ready to adopt a four-legged friend.

Even if you swear to your parents to take full responsibility for the dog, they probably won't believe you. And they're right. A dog isn't a toy that can be left in a box, unattended.

No matter what breed it is, a dog has his own personality, with its qualities and faults. Dogs need their space, and they take up a lot of it, too.

First, you should ask yourself if the circumstances are right for a dog to be happy in yo[ur] home, rather than forcing the issue.

Furthermore, you should learn as much as you can about the behavior of this "carnivore." If dogs feel threatene[d] they defend themselves by attackir[g] and biting, so the decision to adopt [a] dog shouldn't be made on a whim.

A dog lives an average of twelve years. Taking care of him for that long is a big responsibility. Loving him may not be enough. The decision to adopt a dog should be made by the whole family. That way you can avoid any bitter arguments when the dog does his first bad thing. Isn't that right, Spot?

Why do we have to go to bed at night?

Because sleeping well is necessary for living well!

Think about it: We spend a third of our lives sleeping. That means that a sixty-year-old has spent twenty years of his life sleeping! It's hard not to think that all that time was wasted. So what actually happens during the night without our knowledge?

All day, our brains accumulate tons of new information, control all the movements of our bodies, and rummage around deep in our memory banks to recall information that might come in handy to us. That leaves no time for sorting and cleaning.

After hours of work, the brain is exhausted, so it sends signals to us, like itchy eyes or yawns. There's no use fighting it—you have to go to bed! The brain needs to reestablish order. And if we prevent it from doing so, revenge is around the corner: Confusion and comprehension difficulties ensue!

To work well, you must first sleep well . . .

ZZZZ

The amount of sleep a person needs varies, depending on the amount of time his or her brain needs to regroup.

Children are constantly learning, so they need more sleep than adults. A baby needs more than sixteen hours of sleep a day, and about ten hours are sufficient for children aged six to twelve.

You figure it out! What time should you be going to bed?

91

Index
by subject

The earth

The sky

Habits and quirks

Beliefs

Feelings

Life in society

Unusual questions

Daily life

Flowers and fruit

How does the body work?

Animals